Raves and Reviews

"Susan is a great listener and easy to talk to. She sincerely cares, is super supportive and her warmth and positive outlook are inspiring. Susan is able to relate to wanting permanent solutions, not just temporary fixes. I feel like I can talk to her about anything and trust her intuition and guidance."
                              - Laura Schappert, Sedona Virtual Assistant

"Susan is a mover and a shaker. Over the years she has taught me how to motivate my students, both children and adults to see, plan and fulfill their dreams! "
                              - Rita Seretti, Retired California Teacher

"I am always amazed at the creative and positive solutions Susan is able to produce, especially when it comes to business matters. It's like her ideas are just waiting to be used by aspiring entrepreneurs."
                              - Kacelle, The Organizing Woman

"Susan is an experienced life coach with a natural gift to inspire, encourage and build confidence. Partnering with Susan is simple, fun and incredibly productive. She created a path that empowered me to make my business dream a reality! Her creativity and entrepreneurial mindset resulted in powerful networking and marketing strategies, giving my business a competitive edge."
   - Darla McKamey, RN-C, WHNP, President, Healthy Happies

About the Author

Susan F. Moody is a Certified Success, Business and Life Coach who, for over 20 years, has been working with clients of all ages, helping them define their goals, build their dreams, accelerate their results and create richer, more fulfilling lives.

Susan graduated from Mount St. Mary's College in Los Angeles with a degree in Education. Throughout the years, she has held many titles both personally and professionally having worked in small companies and large corporations. She is also a self-proclaimed serial entrepreneur having owned and operated over ten businesses.

Susan has been a sole proprietor, a franchise owner, a business partner, CEO of an LLC and President of an S Corp. Through her companies, she has sold products and services generating multi-millions in sales dollars. She has served on the board for the Small Business Administration's (SBA) Women's Roundtable, been mentioned in Entrepreneur's *Small Business* Magazine and featured on Talk Radio as well as NBC, ABC, CBS, and Fox affiliate television stations.

Susan became a Certified Coach through Coach Training Alliance in 2003 and received a 2nd certification through Life Mastery Institute in 2013. She became a Coach to facilitate and nurture others on their personal path to success. Susan provides coaching, mentoring, workshops and retreats for individuals and groups ready to embrace change.

She is the creator of the **Yes! U Can Success Coaching Program**© and the **Simple C Success System**©, writer of *Ask the Wise Woman* advice column and author of the *4BNU Tween Mentoring Program* and *Cz the Day!* Susan is also a featured coach in Dawn Billing's book *Coaching for Results* and a co-author with Brian Tracy of the soon to be released, *Beat the Curve*.

Susan currently resides with her husband in the Phoenix area and is a member of America's Premier Experts, the Southwest Valley Chamber of Commerce, Networking Phoenix, The Conscious Community, Gals Prepared to Succeed and the Phoenix Chapter of NAWBO.

For enjoyment, Susan spends time by Oak Creek in Sedona, reading, writing, wine tasting and cruising around the world with her family and close friends. For more information on working with Susan or to discuss speaking opportunities:

email: **susan@u-succeed.com**
toll free: 855-U-SUCCEED
website: www.U-SUCCEED.com

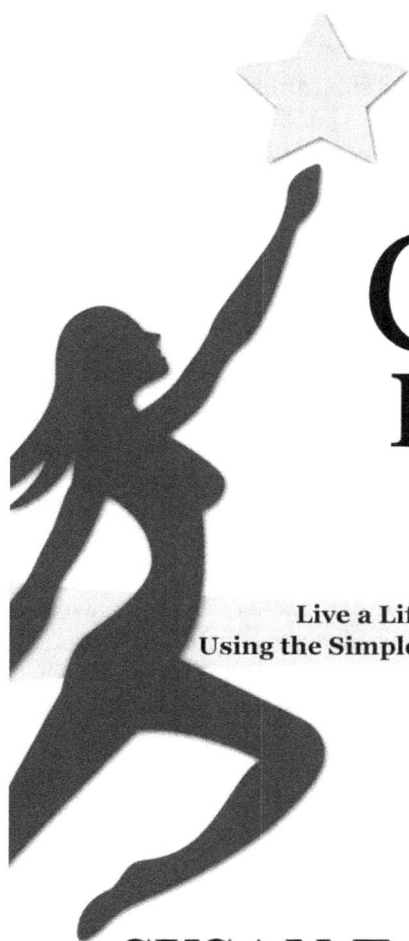

Cz *the* DAY!

**Live a Life You Love:
Using the Simple C Success System©**

SUSAN F. MOODY
Certified Business, Success and Life Coach

"There is only one success – to be able to live your life in your own way." C Morley

Dedication

This book is dedicated to those who have coached and mentored me throughout my life, either knowingly or unknowingly. I have learned just as much, if not more, from the people who have doubted me or said "no" to me, as I have from those of you who have loved me and cheered me on through the years. To all those that did not believe in me or encourage me, you inadvertently inspired me. So, thank you all!

Special Thanks

To my husband, Jim, for once again supporting my creative endeavors and sharing me with this book during our cruise vacations through South America and Alaska.

How to Use this Book

This book has been created for you to read as well as to write in to complete the enclosed exercises. Even though this book is laid out in Modules, you need not necessarily complete the Modules in the order listed in the Table of Contents.

For instance, if you are already very clear on what you want in your life, you might decide to skip Module 1: **CLARITY** and move directly to Module 3: **COURSE** to help you develop your action plan.

It is my sincerest hope that by completing the **Simple C Success System**© you will be well on your way to living a life you love.

Here's to your success! ~ *Susan*

Contents

Simple C
Success Sytem©

CREATION

Introduction

I admit it; I am not a big dreamer. I don't have a bucket list or a wish list. I have a "To Do" list. This is the language that speaks and works for me.

In my experience, a dream fades when you awake. So that equates to "not going to happen". And, in actuality, I do dream at night A LOT; in vivid detail and in color. However, my dreams fade away as soon as I awake. Although sometimes not before my husband learns that he did something to upset me in my dream!

A "wish list" is also terminology that doesn't work for me. It reads "I'd really like to have this or do that, but since I can't afford it if I put in on my wish list maybe someone else will be nice enough to get it for me"; kind of like Santa and my Christmas list. The risk in that is that "Santa" isn't you and the elves might just bring something they think would suit you better.

Cz *the* Day!

No, I like "To Do" lists. Lists that can be checked off when you take the appropriate action. Get a better job; check. Take the kids to Disney World; check. Or even better, since I use a "To Do" list daily, for future activities I like the "One Day I Will" list. Such as:

One Day I will:
- Buy a house
- Drive a Mercedes convertible
- Take a European cruise

If you are like me, you deal with the tangibles in life, things that can be accomplished. I do not place stock in dreams and wishes, I want results. Thinking about things doesn't make them happen, taking action does. And, I am all about doing the work necessary to check the boxes.

Think back to when you were a child. If you were like me, people asked you "What do you want to be when you grow up?" They didn't ask "What do you dream of being? What do you wish for in life? What is on your bucket list?"

And you answered: "I want to be a teacher, a doctor, a rocket scientist, a _____" whatever type of profession that you fancied at the time. The possibilities to children are endless. I personally think that they still are today.

CREATION - Introduction

For instance, years ago this was my list. One day I will:
- Be a teacher
- Have children
- Travel the world

I am happy to say that I have accomplished all those goals. My most recent list looks like this. One day I will:
- Be a writer
- Do work that matters to me
- Help women believe in their own personal power

And here I am a certified business, success and life coach for women writing a book! It is amazing to me the power we have within each of us to manifest the very things that are important to us. When I look back on my life, I try to pinpoint exactly when I realized that I had the power within me, that I had everything I needed to live the life I wanted to live. Because I didn't always feel that way.

Like all of us, I have had good days and bad days, made some good choices and some poor choices, been a victim and a victor, had successes and failures. This book is about my own discovery process and the Simple C Success System© that I developed and use to achieve my personal and professional goals. If you are ready to Cz the Day! and take action, you too can create a life you love using this system.

It all began when I was a little girl . . . .

Chapter 1

My mother recently told me that I was born with a white cull over my head, said to mean a blessed child, a special child. This was unbeknownst to me and I never felt I was treated as the "special" child in the family. I am the second child of four children, the other three being my brothers. Growing up I remember always trying to be "one of the boys". I have the perfect picture in my mind that illustrates that sentiment. Back in the day when superheroes were first popular, and Batman and Robin came on the scene, we were all Batman on Halloween. Now I want you to put this picture in your mind.

My family is Italian and most of my relatives are of a shorter stature. My older brother shared this family trait. I, on the other hand, did not. My next brother was almost two years younger than I, so he was also shorter than me. So here we are all in our Batman costumes with me in the middle looking

like an Amazon compared to my two brothers! Seriously, this is an actual photo in our family album.

I even remember a time when we were out buying our family Christmas tree. My grandfather was a barber and so, you guessed it, I had a short haircut just like my brothers. I like to think I was a "daddy's girl" but here we were on the tree lot when an acquaintance of my dad stopped over to say hello and catch up. I was standing right next to my dad when the other gentleman asks "How many children do you have now?", and when my dad answered "four" the other man says, "All boys, congratulations!" Talk about a blow to my budding self-esteem!!!

I mention these stories solely to illustrate that I did not feel that I led a "charmed" life. In credit to my parents, they did their best not to single out any one child and show any favoritism. Of course, kids being kids, we all had the usual jealousies and petty complaints about "fairness", but all in all, we pretty much got along with each other. Being a "middle" child and the only girl, I do feel that I tended to be more of a peacekeeper than some of my other siblings. (Of course, their story may be a bit different!!)

The other item of note is that as I referenced earlier, my family is Italian. Therefore, our family "discussions" could get loud. My mother's voice especially has the ability to be heard clear down the street. I mention this because of the effect this had on me: (1) I have an aversion to noise, (2) I personally do not shout and (3) I rarely share my opinion on something unless asked; meaning I was a fairly quiet child.

There was also some healthy competition in the family. My dad and brothers were very active in sports and boy scouts. We were (and still are) a family that plays games. I was always included in the sports competitions – basketball, baseball, etc. if I wanted to be (and at that time I was not about to be left out!) and even joined the girl scouts for a short time.

We were all encouraged to do our best in school and get high grades. We all went to the same grammar school, and began to believe that our grades were equivalent to our age ranking at home (Oldest = A student, Next = B student, down the line to my youngest brother = D student). Now, there is some truth to "living up to expectations" as this pretty much was the way our report cards ranked. In fact, I didn't even realize I was "smart" until I went to a high school different from that of my older brother. In my mind, he was always the "smart" one.

Cz the Day!

So, all-in-all, this was my "normal" childhood. I just went about my business trying not to make any waves by doing well in school, working a part-time job and preparing to go to college and move out on my own.

This worked just fine for me until I actually did go off to college . . . .

Chapter 2

The day arrived when it was time for my parents to drop me off at the college dorm. Although I had chosen an in-state university not too far from the house (within 1-2 hours' drive time depending on traffic), I decided to live on campus. Now I had just come from an all-girl college prep high school and was placed in the only co-ed dormitory. This was at the cusp of changing times. Women no longer had to choose between a degree in "husbandry" or teaching, but could explore becoming an engineer, a lawyer, a doctor, whatever their aspiration. So imagine my family's somewhat disappointed sigh when I did indeed want to be a teacher. This is what I always wanted and I still love learning and teaching new skills.

The other big change was my finding a job off campus. My dad wanted me to work on campus, but Little Ms. Independent wanted to make her own way. So I worked part time as a receptionist/secretary (gasp!) at an event company not too far away from the university and to which I could ride my bike. This was before the days when every kid gets their own car as soon as they turn sixteen. And, on my very first day working there, I met my future husband (a hard-working, blue-collar man). Double gasp!!

So suffice it to say that my going off to college was not only a big change for me but an even BIGGER change for my family. Again, I only mention this as background to who I am today. So let's fast forward a few years, married with two children, working at a job where my daughter and son came to work with me, great friends, great house, happy, happy, happy. The only problem was, my husband apparently wasn't. He found "commitment" too restrictive.

So, let's move on to divorce, job change from teaching into the computer industry (i.e. more money), move to a so-so neighborhood – you get the picture. But, these were the days of "I am woman, hear me roar!" So roar I did. I was a quick learner and was soon able to move to a larger company with more pay and benefits, put the kids in private school, buy my own house and carry on just fine by myself; thank you very much.

Until I met the man who would change my life forever. . . .

Chapter 3

I'm sure many of you have heard of the book "Smart Women, Stupid Choices." Well, that was me. Fell totally head over heels with a man who was not only college educated, held a management position, but was totally charming and wined and dined me until I was completely under his spell. Yes, I gave my "power" away to this man. He not only stole my heart, but he stole my money, my friends and family, my self-confidence and made me feel that he "owned" me. In fact, he constantly reminded me that I was "nothing" without him.

By the time I realized that I needed to get out of the relationship, I had already sold my house, moved with him to another state and we were running a business together. It got to the point where I was so out of touch with "me" that I could no longer tell which of us was the crazy person.

When I finally figured out he was definitely making me crazy and I felt it was no longer safe for my kids and me to remain in that environment, I did the one thing most strong-willed, independent people hate to do. . . . I sought out and asked for help.

And, guess what? My friends and family were more than willing to do whatever they could to "rescue" me. They were just waiting for me to ask. Let me tell you that it was a long trek back, literally, since my dad came to drive me and what few possessions I did have left back to the west coast. I had flown the kids to their grandparents for their usual summer vacation and then planned my "escape".

I have to say that since the day I left, I never spoke to that man again; never answered his phone calls, sent back his cards and letters "return to sender." He could keep the house, the boat, the beach house, the business – I just packed up and walked away. Found a new job and vowed "never again". Never again would I be a "victim". Never again will I give my "power" away. Never again would I trust anyone but me to take the best care of me and my children.

Now I just had to re-learn how to be me. . . .

Chapter 4

Back in the day when I first started working in the computer industry, this was the time when companies were evolving. Management was promoting Stephen Covey's "The 7 Habits" series, theories evolved around "Think and Grow Rich" and Nightingale-Conant training. Being exposed to these "new" principles started changing my own thinking practices. Although I had always been a "can do" type of person, I realized that I was mainly just following the "rules" that had been passed down from my parents and a very conventional society. This was when I began to learn that there are other ways to define success.

When I found myself having to start over, I took a position with another computer company; stepping back into a role of which I was comfortable, the newly renamed position of secretary to "Executive Assistant". This was an interesting time for me having just removed myself from

an emotionally abusive relationship, to find myself working with a man who had a very condescending leadership style. In fact, he was a "yeller" – meaning if something wasn't done by one of his subordinates to his satisfaction, he yelled at them to do better and get it done "right".

Now, remember, I was new here and really needed the job, but there was NO WAY I could work for a man who would scream at me. I am not sure where I found the courage, but one night after working there for about a week, I asked if I could speak with my boss before leaving for the night. I then asked him "if there is anything you would like me to do differently, could you please just let me know without raising your voice as I do not respond well to being yelled at"? He silently looked at me for a moment then said, "I do not allow anyone to speak to me this way and tell me what to do!" To which I replied, "And I no longer allow people to yell at me and I would understand if you want to replace me". (Secretly hoping he would do just that!) To my surprise, however, he simply said, "OK agreed" and thus began one of the most important and transformational relationships in my life. We ended up working together and learning from each other over the next seven years.

One of the methods I was using to rebuild my self-confidence was to keep a daily flip calendar on my desk that included an inspirational quote. I remember reading the quote "Destiny is not a matter of chance, it is a matter of choice; it is not a thing to be waited for: it is a thing to be achieved." What a profound impact those words had on me. This became my daily mantra as it reminded me that it is the choices I make that create the life I am living.

Another was "Your attitude is the only thing you can control". You see, these quotes were important to me because I could very easily have become bitter and felt like a victim, due to my recent life experiences. But once I recognized that I could and did make a choice to change my life, this shifted my attitude. I now began to believe that no matter my situation I could still keep a positive, optimistic attitude.

In fact, this is still one of my guiding principles today. Since I cannot go back, but only go forward, I leave the past in the past. I find no value in going back and beating myself up for the choices I made or experiences I have had; they have helped to shape me and who I am.

I just chalk it up to another "life lesson" and move on. . . .

Chapter 5

By the time the computer company I was working for was bought out by a larger company several years later, I had moved up into a management position. One that came with a very nice severance package; the kind that allows one to think about "what would I really like to do". So I started to think about the things I like now and the things I used to like through the years and what I am good at: well, I liked being my own boss, I would like to support people who have their own business, I like to plan meetings and host events, I like getting a massage, having my nails done, I liked having my kids at work with me, I would like the convenience of using all my skills and having the services I need and use in one location.

So, what do I do? I find a location that can house my business idea, find some additional investors, write up a business plan, receive the funding to buy the building and voila! a new "executive suites" business is born. Yes, I know, I make it sound easy here, but to be honest, I found the challenge of being able to pull something like this together fun and exciting (although it scared the heck out of most of my family and friends).

To me, this was just another part of my personal plan to "re-learn" me. To remind myself that I can do anything I set my mind to and it worked. When this business was operational for just a few years, an up and coming new company liked the concept so much, they bought us out to make our building their corporate office.

Which then gave me the opportunity to once again ask myself "What would I like to do next?" . . . .

Chapter 6

Welcome to Coaching! I am an "analytical" by nature (another acknowledgment of the management style of the late 80's) and am quite happy researching all my possibilities. When I was seeking a new profession that focused on helping people (mainly women) tap into their personal power, I looked into becoming a "life coach".

I realized that I had become an enthusiastic advocate of personal development over the years, so this new vocation really appealed to me. I became certified and hung out my shingle, so to speak. Unfortunately for me, I discovered that I had a problem with setting boundaries with my clients. I found that although I enjoyed the work, it was emotionally draining and not as financially rewarding as I had hoped.

Plus, being that I was at the forefront of the coaching "movement" at that time, there was a lot of effort in helping to

gain awareness and creditability to this new profession. In addition to the coaching, I also used some of the profits from my former business to invest in real estate, mainly vacation rental properties. The plan was for us (my new husband and I) to invest in these properties as part of our retirement plan while using these homes for our own family vacations; which is what we did for the next few years.

During this investment time, however, we found a property we really liked for ourselves and decided to move out of state and into this house. This gave me a reasonable, understandable way to shift the nature of my coaching business.

Chapter 7

Although I chose to suspend my coaching practice practice for the time being, I still continued to be interested, study, learn and practice the principles of the power of our thoughts. Over the years, I have watched how Oprah, Tony Robbins, Dwayne Dyer and many others have increased the awareness of these "law of attraction" principles. So once we moved, I again began to look for my "what next" project.

Our area was relatively new and did not have a lot of nice independent restaurants or wine bars. One of the shared activities my husband and I have is wine tasting. So, off I go exploring owning and operating my own restaurant. I take classes in restaurant management, bartending, health codes, etc. Find a location, write up a business plan, sought and receive financing and voila! open an upscale restaurant. And it did great . . . for the first year and a half, before the recession hit. Then, the bottom fell out. We, like a lot of others, took a major hit to our finances – not only losing the restaurant, but our investment properties and even my husband's 401k was affected.

Yep, this was a major blow to me personally. I am the woman who prided herself on always having a backup plan and who had no backup plan in place. Oh, how the mighty had fallen!! And let me tell you, there was no one harder on me than me. So, now what??

There was no way I felt I could start another business right away and I really, really, really did not want a traditional 8-5 job, but I knew I needed to bring an income into the household. So, the Research Queen got online and started exploring her options. What could a former teacher with a high level of computer skills and management experience do?

Well, it was the dawning of government mandated electronic health records. And, there were lots of software companies getting into this new industry. I found a company that if I was willing to pay to become certified in their software they would bring me on as an independent contractor to train their clients on their product and compensate me at a pretty good hourly rate plus travel expenses.

Now, some people may not have been excited by this opportunity (having no money to pay up front and no guarantee of work upon completion of training), but I like a challenge and thought that this may just be something I was good at and enjoy.

So, I find a way to come up with the money and off I went. Although this position involved quite a bit of travel, I found that I did indeed enjoy training others and was doing a good enough job that the corporate office offered me my own business alliance partnership within the first few years. Of course, I first had to put together a business plan for them to review, which they thought might intimidate me (little did they know!).

So I jumped right on that bandwagon and once again had my own business. You see life is like that. If you are willing to say "yes" when an opportunity arrives, you might just be surprised where life takes you.

Chapter 8

After several years of riding the wave of EMR software training, the company I was in partnership with got bought out; just as they had planned it. Since I had been through another corporate buyout years earlier I knew just what to expect - changes, BIG changes. So I thought, here it comes another "What do I want to do next?" moment.

Back when I had started my coaching business I had put together some worksheets and activities for my clients to use to help them discover what I call their "SOUL" Goal™. That objective that aligns their Sense of Purpose, Own Values, Unique Talents, and Life's Passion. What better way, I thought, than to use my own self-discovery tool, to figure out what I want to do. This process once again led me to coaching. I am very passionate about helping others achieve the success they desire in their life. Once this fire was re-ignited, I wanted to refresh my skills and became re-certified.

This time, when I was seeking a certification program I was looking for one that specialized in focusing on the whole person and transformational coaching. One I felt would embody all the principles I believe in and practice as well as help establish a foundational training program for my clients, and one that focuses on running a successful coaching business as well as being a good coach and mentor.

Through my new certification program, I found that not only was coaching now accepted as a viable industry but that marketing methods had changed. I learned that I had to be involved in social media. Now I have mentioned that I am a pretty quiet, very private person, so I had not been interested in joining Facebook, LinkedIn, etc. However, I had discovered that having a business today almost requires that you participate in having a social media presence.

I also found that to build my business I would have to do public speaking. This program felt very strongly that speaking is the ideal way to meet potential clients. Yep, I have a fear of this along with a lot of other people. So much so that when I speak, I have to "trick my mind" and tell myself that I am just teaching a class – something I have been doing for years!!

Some people say that I give the impression of being fearless because I am willing to try something new. Well, this is absolutely not true. For example, here are the two very things that so far I had been able to avoid (by choice) and now I find that I should do both to build my new business. Of course, I still have the choice whether I do these things or not, but my desire to build a successful coaching practice outweighs my reluctance, so I do them anyway!!

Chapter 9

You may remember that my current "One Day I Will" list looks like this
- Be a writer
- Do work that matters to me
- Help women believe in their own personal power

Coaching and empowering women from middle-school through mid-life is work that matters to me. Writing is one of the tools I use to help women of any age believe in their own personal power. You may have picked up that I don't like to talk about myself, that I am a pretty private person and that I don't typically give my opinion unless asked. Yet, here is a book that so far is mainly about me and my personal development.

I share this story of my life simply as a way to illustrate that I am the same as you. To point out that I have had some bad days, made some poor choices, been a victim

and had failures in the past and will probably experience all of these again in my future. But, that doesn't stop me from moving forward. That doesn't stop me from still wanting to have a "One Day I Will List" and working on my list.

In the next part of this book introduction, I would like to share with you my personal philosophy on coaching and my Simple C Success System© along with some of the tools that you, like me, can use to keep inspired and motivated to check off your own boxes.

Chapter 10

Just as there are lots of doctors, lawyers, accountants and other professionals for you to choose from, there are tons of coaches. Some are certified; some are not. Some follow the guiding principles of their mentors and some follow their own principles. It is important when you choose to work with a coach, you choose someone that you trust and connect with. Not all coaches are for everyone. You should select one that matches up with your personal needs of a coach. For instance, you wouldn't choose to go to a pediatrician when you are expecting a child, for that you choose to see an obstetrician.

My personal philosophy of coaching centers on my clients definition of success. Most people would choose to be viewed as a success rather than as a failure. But, each person's definition of success can be very different. There is the traditional definition tied very closely to financial success or there is the non-traditional definition of success tied to inner peace and harmony. Whatever your personal definition is of success that is what I want for you as well.

I have long ago severed ties with tradition. To me, success isn't all about the money. Don't get me wrong, I like having money – enough money to support myself and my family and to have some "fun money". I never like having to "rob Peter to pay Paul" when writing out the monthly bills. I don't like having to turn down dinner with friends because I can't afford to go out to eat. I simply want to have enough money to do what I want to do, when I want to do it!

To me, success isn't about owning the nicest house on the block. It is about providing a stable, home environment in a safe neighborhood for my family – regardless of whether I am renting or mortgaging the monthly payment.

To me, success is not being a corporate executive working 60-80 hours per week to prove my value to the company. It is doing work that matters to me and having the flexibility to do the things I want to be doing with the people I love the most.

To me, success isn't being a size extra small and having to watch what I eat and exercise constantly to fit in those clothes. It is being healthy, feeling good in my body and having enough energy to participate in the activities that I enjoy.

Now, remember, this is how I define success. Not necessarily YOU. However, what I find working with my clients is that it is much easier to say "I don't want this" than to define "I do want this".

If this sounds like you, the "not quite knowing" exactly what you want, just that you want something more or different than what you have, you will want to work with a coach that can help you clarify your personal definition of success.

Chapter 11

The first module of the Simple C Success System© is CLARITY – knowing your personal and professional goals as they relate to the four main areas of your life. Here is an exercise to get you started.

Think through each of these areas and jot down your answers to these questions:

1) Health and Well-Being
   a. Are you at your ideal weight?
   b. Are you able to participate in the physical activities you enjoy?
   c. Do you maintain a healthy diet?
   d. How do you feel in your body?
   e. Do you dress for success?

2) Love and Relationships
   a. Are you surrounded by your friends and family?
   b. Is there any discord that needs to be resolved?
   c. Are you longing for a deep, loving relationship?
   d. Do you need to forgive yourself?
   e. Do you love yourself as much as you love others?

3) Career and Vocation
   a. How do you see yourself expressing your gifts?
   b. Have you moved up the corporate ladder?
   c. Are you running your own business?
   d. Are you participating in creative arts?
   e. What would you be happy doing?

4) Time and Money Freedom
   a. How much money do you want to be making?
   b. What would you do with that money?
   c. Where are you living?
   d. What are you doing with your time?
   e. How could you enjoy your life more?

So, how do you define success? I encourage you to write it down on the next page.

My definition of success is:

Chapter 12

I have found that even if you are very clear on what you want, if you haven't really analyzed why you want what you want and what makes this goal important to you, you can easily get distracted from achieving the results you desire. In order to move forward with CONFIDENCE you need to know who you are and your CORE VALUES.

Spend some time and write down a few things that are truly important to you. For instance, some of the things I value are:
- Spending quality time with my family and friends
- Serving a purpose that matters to me

Write the things that matter the most to you below:

_____

_____

_____

_____

Now, take a moment and review your definition of success. Does this definition align with your core values? If not, you may want to go back and redefine your overall vision.

Chapter 13

Now, once you know what you want and why you want it then you have to figure out how to get it. I work with some clients that have a very clear vision of what they want their life to be, yet feel stuck with the life they are currently living. These clients need a clear **COURSE** to follow. They need an action plan to move them from where they are today to where they want to be.

For instance, if one of my goals is to live in a nicer neighborhood within 6 months then I would need to break down this goal into small steps. If I keep telling myself that I can never afford to move to a nicer area, then guess what? I won't ever move. If, however, I start detailing it out I stand a very good chance of making it happen.

For instance:
    Goal: Move to a Nicer Neighborhood
    Deadline: within 6 months

Cz the Day!

Step 1: Research prices of homes in nicer neighborhoods
Step 2: Figure out how to raise/save enough money for the security deposit or down payment
Step 3: Figure out finances to pay for rent/mortgage
Step 4: Find a house that fits my determined budget
Step 5: Rent/buy a house and move in.

Now, I know what some of you are thinking. And, I agree, it is not as simple as just writing down these steps. But, I guarantee that by writing the steps you have shifted your thoughts from thinking "this is an impossible goal" to thinking "hmm, maybe I can make a move". Once you open your mind to the possibilities, you will be amazed at your own creativity.

Now that you have your basic outline, you then start breaking down the steps even further until you have a very manageable and plausible plan. For example:

Step 1: Research prices of homes in nicer neighborhoods
Deadline: within 1 month
   a) Average price of home: $800-$900/mo
   b) Size of home: 3 bedroom
   c) Distance to Schools: within 10 min
   d) Commute time: with 30 min
   e) Make decision of which area to move to

CREATION - Chapter 13

Then once you have your overall plan, you work the plan. Now at this point I frequently hear "Susan, if I knew what to do, don't you think I'd be doing it?" Well, not necessarily, and I'll tell you why.

Then once you have your overall plan, you work the plan. Now at this point I frequently hear "Susan, if I knew what to do, don't you think I'd be doing it?" Well, not necessarily, and I'll tell you why.

Chapter 14

I f you have **CLARITY** of what you want, the **CONFIDENCE** to know why you want what you want, and a **COURSE** for how to achieve it, then why are you not going for it? This is your time to **Cz the Day!** Unfortunately, this is where those old "fear factors" come into play, or lack of **COURAGE**. Yes, it can be a scary process. And, yes, you are going to run into those people that doubt that you can have what you want. Believe me I have experienced this first hand many times. But, so what??

What is the worst thing that can happen? And this is a question you seriously need to ask yourself. If you really want to open your own business, but if the worst thing that could happen is the business fails (not YOU, but the business) and you can live with this outcome because you would later regret never having tried working for yourself, then you go for it. If the worst thing that could happen is that you would lose your investment and you could not

live with this outcome, because you would regret that you lost your savings then this is not the opportunity for you. You go back and seek further **CLARITY**. Maybe you research a different type of business with less financial impact. Whatever, but you keep moving forward.

Not all of the businesses I have started have turned out to be a commercial success, but some have. Do I regret starting those businesses, surprisingly no. Because I like the challenge and the thrill of trying something new, it makes me feel alive. Now did I take some big financial hits, yes. Did I take some bigger emotional hits, oh yes. Did I find out that friends and family are not always your best support team? Sure, but isn't it always easier to be the one that plays it safe and has the opportunity to say "I told you so", than to be the risk taker?

And, here is the good news, I have always, (yes, always) been able to recover financially. I just go back to "What do I want to do next?" and start the process all over again. I personally want to feel that I have truly lived a happy, fulfilled life rather than having just made it "safely" to my death.

So the bigger question may be to ask yourself this, if at the end of your life would you regret that you didn't do ____? (start that business, adopt that child, travel through Europe) whatever it is you desire. If your answer is "yes" then maybe you should do it while you can.

Chapter 15

The road to success is not always easy. You will almost always run into some forks in the road; possibly even some serious roadblocks. This is where your COMMITMENT plays a very important role. Remember what we talked about before, if you want something bad enough, you will figure out a way to get it. But it is just as true that sometimes it is easy to give up when the going gets tough. So on those days when it seems that you are taking two steps forward only to move three steps back, remind yourself of your "why" and re-commit to yourself and your goals.

There is always something you can do today that will be a step in the direction of your dream. And here's another secret, you may just discover a different path along your way that will get you to the place you wanted to be quicker; or even find a place you want to stop and visit for a while.

Cz the Day!

We've all heard that "it is not the destination, it is the journey that is important". So enjoy your journey. If you are not finding any joy and happiness along the way, maybe you should seek further clarity.

And, lastly, most successful people do not go it alone. If you do not have a built-in support team in place, consider hiring a **COACH** who can help you gain the confidence you need to move forward and be your accountability partner. This is the main reason I became a certified coach and mentor. I have seen the difference it can make in a person's life when they have someone who will believe in them, inspire them, empower them and mentor them to success.

Conclusion

The main thing I have learned through my re-discovering process is that to gain my heart's desire – my definition of success – I had to lose my old self; some part of my old life. And, to do this, I had to have courage because without it I could not have made the leap; the leap of faith to complete that "one day I will" list.

And it did not happen overnight. I didn't just wake up one day and make the leap. I started with "what if" inquiries and took small steps to test the waters while I was building up my courage. Every small step I took when successful, worked on boosting my confidence. Every step that failed made me relook at the action taken and try a different approach.

Sometimes I ran into a lot of "no's" before I heard my first "yes". But this I know for sure, there is always a solution to every situation. And hearing a "no" actually inspires and challenges me to figure it out. I have found that this is one of my natural talents. So much so, in fact, that my husband sometimes cautions friends to be sure about what they want before they tell me, because my drive to figure out how you can get it automatically kicks in. This is where the "be careful what you wish for" phrase comes into play.

And, I don't think I am the only one with this ability. I believe you have it within you as well. When you want something strongly enough, you will figure out how to get it. When you were a young child, it may have been asking dad if mom said no. Growing up you might have traded one thing you had for something one of your friends had that you wanted more. You may have worked overtime, so you could afford to go on that weekend getaway. The same principle works on your bigger goals as well.

You just have to know what you want, why you want it, figure out how you get it, be willing to take the necessary actions and have a support system to help you achieve your goals. **The Simple C Success System©: Clarity, Confidence, Course, Courage, Commitment, Coach.** At least this is what has worked for me and I would encourage you to try it for yourself.

The remainder of this book is broken down into six modules, one for each C in the Success System. Each of these modules will take you step-by-step through exercises to create the life you would love to live. Feel free to go through the modules in whatever order makes sense to you. You only have one life, make it a life worth living. **Cz the Day!** - *Susan*

Cz the Day!

One Day I Will:

_____

_____

_____

_____

_____

Simple C Success System©

Clarity: Know how you define success and what
             goals are important to you.

Confidence: Identify who you are, your core values, and
             be sure your goals are in alignment.

Course: Develop an action plan with the steps and
             deadlines needed to accomplish your goals.

Courage: Be able to ask for the help you need or do
             what scares you anyway.

Commitment: Come up with solutions to situations as they
             arise. Figure out a way to make it happen.

Coach: Have someone who believes in you, inspires
             you, empowers you and mentors you to
             success!

Module 1

CLARITY

Introduction

Nobody wants to feel like they have failed in life. But what exactly is failure? Most likely you feel like you have failed when you have let someone down or disappointed yourself. One of my favorite quotes is "the only thing you can control is your attitude". And to me, a failure is just that, an attitude. Just like success is all about your attitude or outlook on life.

Now you and I are both familiar with the conventional symbols of success (nice house, luxury car, expensive toys, etc.), but if that is not how you personally define success you will find yourself still disappointed with life once you have obtained these material possessions.

I believe the key is to get very clear on what it is that matters to you and, more importantly, why. If your drive to live in the best neighborhood is only because that is where your friends live ("keeping up with the Joneses"), you may feel constantly pressured to live a lifestyle outside of your means; causing you to buy a new car when they buy a new car, join them on a vacation to Europe etc. – do things that you would not normally do, to keep up a certain "appearance".

If, however, your drive to live in the best neighborhood is because this is where the school system you want your children to attend is located, then your focus is on your family needs. You would not feel pressured to purchase a new car if one is not needed or go on a vacation to Europe when your family would prefer a Disney World vacation.

My process for achieving Success is through using the **Simple C Success System©: Clarity, Confidence, Course, Courage, Commitment, Coach.** In this module we are going to explore **CLARITY**: knowing how you define success, what goals are important to you and why.

Chapter 1

The first phase of becoming successful is **CLARITY:** knowing how you define success. For many of us, the first thought that comes to mind relates to the conventional status symbols of success which all have to do with money, money and more money. Although I like the things that money can buy me, money is not the driving force in my life. Instead of saying one day when I have money, I will take the kids to Disney World. I say, I would like to take the kids to Disney World, how can I make enough money to take us all there?

This is a mind shift. I am opening my mind to the possibility that I will be able to take that family vacation. You know how when you were growing up and really, really wanted something, instead of your parents saying "no" they told you "maybe"? Well, this is similar to that. Yes, I know what you are thinking, "but my parents really did mean no, when they said maybe!" But, before you figured that out, didn't you have hope that a yes could be forthcoming?

At this point, I just want you to be open to a "maybe". Say to yourself that maybe what I really want in life can happen for me. Because I have to tell you right now, if you don't think it can happen, it probably won't. What is that famous saying by Henry Ford? "Whether you think you can or you think you can't, you are right!"

In order to get clear on what it is you really want and how you define success, you have to believe in your mind that you can have it and in your heart that you deserve it. So, let's get you started on coming up with your definition of success.

Chapter 2

I n this exercise you are going to start determining what you really want as it relates to four main areas of your life. Now during this exercise, do not limit your thoughts based on whether you think something is achievable or not. You are simply putting down what it is you desire in these four areas. Think through each of these areas and jot down your answers to these questions:

1) Health and Well-Being
    a. Are you at your ideal weight?
    b. Are you able to participate in the physical activities you enjoy?
    c. Do you maintain a healthy diet?
    d. How do you feel in your body?
    e. Do you dress for success?
    f. What is it you would love to have in regards to your Health and Well Being?

Answer below:

_____

_____

_____

_____

2) Love and Relationships
   a. Are you surrounded by your friends and family?
   b. Is there any discord that needs to be resolved?
   c. Are you longing for a deep, loving relationship?
   d. Do you need to forgive yourself?
   e. Do you love yourself as much as you love others?
   f. What is it you would love to have in regards to Love and Relationships? Answer below:

_____

_____

_____

_____

3) Career and Vocation
   a. How do you see yourself expressing your gifts?
   b. Have you moved up the corporate ladder?
   c. Are you running your own business?

d.   Are you participating in creative arts?
e.   What would you be happy doing?
f.   What is it you would love to have in regards to your Career and Vocation? Answer below:

_____

_____

_____

_____

4)   Time and Money Freedom
a.   How much money do you want to be making?
b.   What would you do with that money?
c.   Where are you living?
d.   What are you doing with your time?
e.   How could you enjoy your life more?
f.   What is it you would love to have in regards to your Time and Money Freedom? Answer below:

_____

_____

_____

_____

So, now that you are a little more clear on exactly what you would love to be doing, re-write how you define success below:.

My definition of success is:

_____

_____

_____

_____

Chapter 3

When I first began to explore my personal definition of success, it was an emotional experience for me. I felt I was finally getting in tune with what is important to me; not my family, not my friends, not my business associates but me. Although on one hand it felt quite liberating, on the other it felt a bit scary. I knew that if I wanted to follow my own path, I would face criticism of my choices and pessimism about my abilities.

There are always going to be pessimists in this world. People who look at the downside of situations and never have anything positive to say. I cannot stress enough that this has everything to do with them and practically nothing to do with you. If they cannot fathom themselves doing the very thing you are striving to do then it must just not be possible for anyone.

Cz the Day!

Most of us grew us with similar platitudes: "It takes money you don't have to do that!", "Money doesn't grow on trees", "You already have everything you need, why do you want more?", "Why can't you just be happy with what you have?". Well I say it is time to throw out those old TAPES (things that Take Away your Power, Energy and Sense of Self) and create your own DVD (Destiny with Vision and Determination). Success does not happen overnight. It takes time. It takes patience. It is going to take everything you've got. But you are willing to give it because success is important to you.

I have found that sometimes it helps me to deflect others pessimism and not take it quite as personally if I take a moment and anticipate their concerns and consider how I might respond.

Chapter 4

Here is an exercise I sometimes use to help turn a negative into a positive. In my experience, no one will understand your motivation and drive to achieve the success you desire as well as you. And most concerns that others will have for you are based on their own doubts. So, in order to best respond, their concerns need to be eased.

Here are a few examples from my own life:

Their Question:

> Are you really sure you want to leave your job to start your own business?

The Underlying Concern:

> What happens if the business fails and you are left without a job (i.e. a source of income).

Cz the Day!

My Response:
> I understand the risks involved with starting my own business, but worse case I can always find another job. In fact, I've already talked to my boss, and although my same position might not be available, she has assured me that I would always be welcome back.

Their Question:
> Can you really afford to take that European cruise?

The Underlying Concern:
> Either they can't afford it themselves or feel it is a frivolous expense.

My Response:
> Yes, this is something I've been saving towards for a while and I am so excited!

> I invite you to try this exercise. If nothing else, you can list your own questions, concerns and responses to put yourself in a more positive, can-do attitude.

The Question:

_____

_____

The Underlying Concern:

_____

_____

Your Response:

_____

_____

The Question:

_____

_____

Cz the Day!

The Underlying Concern:

_____

_____

Your Response:

_____

_____

Conclusion

U sing the Simple C Success System© you have just delved into C = **CLARITY.** By completing the included exercises, you will have thought about and written down your goals enhancing the **CLARITY** of what you want in your life.

It is my hope that you are clear on what it is you really want and your personal definition of success; and that you are excited about the possibilities. Now let's work on building up your Confidence so that you truly believe that you can change your life and have your heart's desire.

Module 2

CONFIDENCE

Introduction

Perhaps at this point in the **CLARITY** process, you are realizing that there is more to life; more joy, more happiness, more money, more fulfillment. You know there is and the ideas are flowing. There is a nagging tug in the corner of your mind telling you to go out there and do it. Be all that you can be. Believe in yourself. You want to, you really want to – but before you go out and do "it" – you want to be really sure that the ultimate goal you have set for yourself answers that burning question "Why am I here?"

I call this your Soul Goal™: that objective that aligns your Sense of Purpose, Own Values, Unique Talents and Life's Passion. For me, it is all well and good to work towards my definition of success, but my underlying desire is to live a life I love serving a purpose that matters to me. So I went on a quest to figure out my purpose; which lead me to create the following exercise. When you are in sync with who you are and your core values, this is what truly gives you **CONFIDENCE.**

Chapter 1

What is My Soul Goal™?

Step 1:   Find yourself a quiet spot where you can take about 30 minutes of uninterrupted time.

Step 2:   Close your eyes and take some deep breaths to clear your mind.

Step 3:   For each question write down the first answers that come to mind. Do not censor yourself. There is no right or wrong answer. This is about YOU.

Cz the Day!

Write down up to (10) words that describe you:

1. _____

2. _____

3. _____

4. _____

5. _____

6. _____

7. _____

8. _____

9. _____

10. _____

Write down up to (10) words that describe what is important to you:

1. _____

2. _____

3. _____

4. _____

5. _____

6. _____

7. _____

8. _____

9. _____

10. _____

Write down up to (10) words that describe what you are good at doing:

1. _____

2. _____

3. _____

4. _____

5. _____

6. _____

7. _____

8. _____

9. _____

10. _____

Write down up to (10) words that describe what you would really want to do:

1. _____

2. _____

3. _____

4. _____

5. _____

6. _____

7. _____

8. _____

9. _____

10. _____

Step 4: Go back through each of these lists and rank them in order of importance based on the assumption that you only have five years to live.

Step 5: Using the top choices from each list, complete the following:

I am a _____

who values _____ in me and

others. Using my_____ skills, my

Soul Goal™ is _____.

Here is how this exercise turned out for me: (I have bolded the ones I prioritized from step 4)

Write down up to (10) words that describe you:

confident	smart	witty
creative	compassionate	loving
dedicated	introspective	**intuitive**
driven		

Cz the Day!

Write down up to (10) words that describe what is important to you:

integrity	creativity	**respect**
inner harmony	thoughtfulness	intelligence
generosity	peaceful	self-reliance
optimism		

Write down up to (10) words that describe what you are good at doing:

organizing	**strategizing**	planning
teaching	helping	computer skills
driven	business	creative thinking

Write down up to (10) words that describe what you would really want to do:

empower women	help others
relax	**spend more time with family**

I am a creative, confident, intuitive woman who values integrity, respect and optimism in myself and others. Using my organizing, strategizing and teaching skills, my Soul Goal™ is to help empower other women while spending more time with my family.

Chapter 2

I admit it felt good, very good, to finally have a real sense of my purpose. Now I was ready to get down to the heart and soul of the matter. Why is my definition of success important to me? It is great to have goals, big goals, but I have found that unless you are emotionally attached to the goal you will not have the drive and tenacity to achieve them.

Earlier I mentioned the example of having the goal to live in the "best" neighborhood. If my why was because this is where all my friends live, then that may or may not be enough of a driving factor for me to move there. Or, it could be, but I would be putting an unnecessary financial strain on the family budget because I really cannot afford to be living there. And, then every time my friends have a spectacularly expensive birthday party for their child, I feel the need to compete with them and have an even better party for my child.

This could result in a never-ending vicious cycle that does not equate to a happy, fulfilled life. On the other hand, it could be just the push I need to live that lifestyle. I find that checking my definition of success relative to my Soul Goal™ helps me clarify if the two are in sync. In this example, if I have to work 80 hours a week to afford to live in this neighborhood, then this would decrease the amount of time I have available to spend with my family. So I would then be out of alignment and should perhaps reconsider living in the "best" neighborhood and choose living in a "better" neighborhood somewhat close to work so I can attend my children's school and sports activities.

Chapter 3

S o let's further explore your goals that make up your definition of success. Why is each one important to you? How will it make you feel when you achieve that goal? If you are not significantly attached to your objective, it is harder to stay motivated to do the work necessary to achieve the goal. So, think about what is the real driver behind each of your goals that you listed in Module 1, Chapter 2.

HEALTH AND WELL-BEING GOAL:

_____

_____

_____

Why is this goal Important to you?

_____

_____

_____

Cz the Day!

How will you feel when you achieve this goal?

_____

_____

_____

LOVE AND RELATIONSHIPS GOAL:

_____

_____

_____

Why is this goal Important to you?

_____

_____

_____

How will you feel when you achieve this goal?

_____

_____

_____

CAREER AND VOCATION GOAL:

_____

_____

_____

Why is this goal Important to you?

_____

_____

_____

How will you feel when you achieve this goal?

_____

_____

_____

TIME AND MONEY FREEDOM GOAL:

_____

_____

_____

Cz the Day!

Why is this goal Important to you?

_____

_____

_____

How will you feel when you achieve this goal?

_____

_____

_____

Chapter 4

Now that you are in tune with your Soul Goal™ and have further clarified what you want in the four main areas of your life, it may be necessary to revise your definition of success. The clearer you can be on what it is you want in your life, the better your chances of achieving it. For instance, instead of writing "I want a better paying job", put down "I want a job as a _____ in the _____ industry making $_____."

My definition of success is:

_____

_____

_____

_____

Chapter 5

So far you have thought about your goals and written them down, now you need a visual reminder of your goals. The clearer you can visualize what you want in life, the more real the possibility becomes. One of the ways to do this is to create a vision board. You can choose to do this either by using tangible materials or online. I personally prefer using magazine images and supplementing with online images.

So here is what I do. I gather up my favorite magazines, put on my favorite music and find myself a comfortable spot. I then take my time and browse through the magazines, not to read the articles, but to cut out any pictures I like or words that have meaning for me. I don't question my choices I simply let the images pile up.

When I am done, I make a collage of these clippings in a way that is pleasing to me. I am the only one that needs to be

happy with the result. Then I step back and really look at my collage to reflect on what I see. Is there a recurrent theme? What I find is that all the images and words I chose consciously or subconsciously visually reflected my goals. For instance, my very first collage had a picture of an Adirondack chair on a beach, an airplane, and the word "writer".

A few months ago, when I was doing some "spring cleaning" in my office, I came across this collage behind one of the file cabinets. I truly had forgotten I had put it there. When I took a look at it, I realized that all the images I had selected had come true for me. I had a beach home, I had done a lot of traveling and I had written a book. . . . this was just another example of the power of our thoughts.

I prefer working with the actual magazines, but you can also choose images online and create a virtual vision board. The important thing is to have your vision board be visible, either physically on a wall or as your computer wallpaper.

Chapter 6

know creating this vision board may sound trivial and one you may choose to skip, but I encourage you to try it. Everyone learns differently. Some are audio learners, some learn through reading, and some are visual learners. Here is a simplified outline of what your vision board could look like:

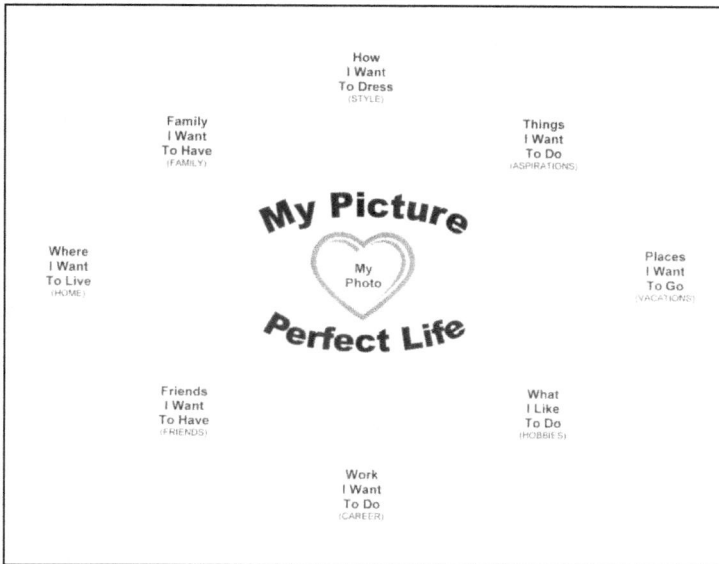

How
I Want
To Dress
(STYLE)

Family
I Want
To Have
(FAMILY)

Things
I Want
To Do
(ASPIRATIONS)

Where
I Want
To Live
(HOME)

My Picture

My
Photo

Places
I Want
To Go
(VACATIONS)

Perfect Life

Friends
I Want
To Have
(FRIENDS)

What
I Like
To Do
(HOBBIES)

Work
I Want
To Do
(CAREER)

Conclusion

By identifying your Soul Goal™, you have melded together who you are and your values with the life you want to create for yourself. You should now feel very CONFIDENT that you can change your life and have your heart's desire.

I remember after going through this clarity process thinking, "Well this is great. I know what I want but have no clue how I am going to get it." Well that, my friends, is C = COURSE

Module 3

COURSE

Introduction

I am not a conventional thinker. I don't put much stock in the status quo symbols of success. I am all about achieving those goals that make up my definition of success. Yes, I have a "One Day" list, make at least one New Year's resolution and keep a vision board. But, just wanting something doesn't make it happen. I need a plan. I need a clear COURSE to follow that will get me from where I am today to where I want to be.

Just mentioning that conjures up anxiety and confusion. It seems an overwhelming task to come up with a plan. I mean, if I knew how to get to where I wanted to be, wouldn't I just get up and go? Sometimes, yes – but sometimes no. If I want to go to the grocery store, I know how to get there since I have been there before. If I want to go to New York, I may have to look up my options for getting there as there will be multiple routes.

The same is true in life. There will be different routes you can take, but you will want to start with your initial itinerary in mind. This, of course, does not mean you cannot take a side trip if you decide along the way you have come across something of interest that you would like to visit in route to your final destination.

Yes, yes I know "it is not the destination, it is the journey". But I prefer my journey to begin with a destination in mind. And that is what we will explore in this module. How to establish your COURSE of action so you can create your own path to the success you desire.

Now let's begin. . . .

Chapter 1

If you have been following the **Simple C Success System©,** you may have completed the 1st C of Success = CLARITY and the 2nd: CONFIDENCE. The exercises in these modules walked you through how to clearly state your definition of success and to create your overall goals in the four main areas of your life: Health and Well-Being, Love and Relationships, Career and Vocation, Time and Money Freedom.

The third phase of becoming successful is creating a **COURSE:** developing an action plan with the steps and deadlines needed to accomplish your goals. In this module, your definition of success will be considered your destination, and you will use the same goals to chart your course. If you have not completed Modules 1and 2, I encourage you to do so now.

Cz the Day!

In order to continue with this module, please take a moment and answer the following:

My definition of success is:

_____

_____

_____

_____

My top (3) goals for the next year are: (in order of priority)

1) _____

2) _____

3) _____

Chapter 2

Got it? Good! Now it is time to put on your thinking cap; time to figure out exactly what you will need in order to achieve your goals. With this exercise, you are not going to get into who, what, when, cost, etc. of each line item to complete, you will just be making a "To Do" list of things that need to be completed.

I understand that a list (especially a long list) can seem overwhelming, but that is what this module is about; how to develop a manageable plan. At this point, you are simply going to get everything out of your head and onto paper.

For example, if my #1 Goal is to "Buy a House" I feel I would need to:
- Have a better paying job
- Determine where I want to live
- Clean up my credit

- Have a down payment
- Find a neighborhood within 10 minutes of school
- Figure out a second source of income
- Etc.

Choose one (1) of your goals right now and make your list using the worksheet on the next page. Again, write down all the things that you can think of no matter how improbable you feel the possibility would be for that item to actually happen. Do not worry about having them in any order, just free flow your thoughts onto the page.

Goal "To Do" List

GOAL: _____

TO DO LIST:

1) _____

2) _____

3) _____

4) _____

5) _____

6) _____

7) _____

8) _____

9) _____

10) _____

11) _____

12) _____

If you have more items, feel free to use another sheet of paper.

Chapter 3

Does your list seem daunting? Are you exhausted yet excited at the same time? Take a deep breath. Know that you can do it. Anything worth achieving seems at times impossible. But you are determined to make it happen and know that this goal is important to you and why.

Remember in the CLARITY module we discussed that in order for you to have the tenacity to pursue your SOUL Goal™, you need to be emotionally tied to your definition of success. This would be a good time to remind yourself of the reason(s) that achieving your goal is important to you.

I never said that the Simple **C Success System**© was easy, just that the process is simple. Now let's move on to the next step – sorting your "To Do" list. Take a look at your overall list with an objective eye. Are there some common themes amongst the many items?

Cz the Day!

If we go back to my example, I already see that there are (3) common themes:

1) INCOME (MONEY)
   a. Have a better paying job
   b. Figure out a second source of income
2) LOAN QUALIFICATION (OTHER)
   a. Down payment requirements
   b. Clean up my credit
3) HOME SELECTION (RESEARCH)
   a. Determine where I want to live
   b. Find a neighborhood within 10 minutes of school

Take some time and look over your list. What are your common 3-5 themes? Make a notation by each of your line items indicating an overall category. For instance R=Research, S=Support, E=Education, M=Money, O=Other. Please complete this step before moving on to Chapter 4.

Chapter 4

Now let's organize your Goal "To Do" List by categories. Move items from your master list into the appropriate category (add more lines if needed).

CATEGORY #1: RESEARCH / OR _____

a. _____

b. _____

c. _____

d. _____

e. _____

Cz the Day!

CATEGORY #2: MONEY / OR _____

    a. _____

    b. _____

    c. _____

    d. _____

    e. _____

CATEGORY #3: EDUCATION / OR _____

    a. _____

    b. _____

    c. _____

    d. _____

    e. _____

CATEGORY #4: SUPPORT / OR _____

    a. _____

    b. _____

c. _____

d. _____

e. _____

CATEGORY #5: OTHER OR _____

a. _____

b. _____

c. _____

d. _____

e. _____

Chapter 5

When you have completed that task, you are now ready to prioritize the list by number in the sequence you might complete them. For example:

HOME SELECTION (RESEARCH)
      a. Determine where I want to live
      b. Find a neighborhood within 10 minutes of school

In this example, finding a house within 10 minutes of school will help determine which areas I should research, so I would prioritize as follows:

HOME SELECTION (RESEARCH)
      1. Find a neighborhood within 10 minutes of school
      2. Determine where I want to live

Cz the Day!

As you are working through these exercises, you are continuing to break down your overall goal into manageable steps. Sort your categories now by priority.

CATEGORY #1: RESEARCH / OR _____

1) _____

2) _____

3) _____

4) _____

5) _____

CATEGORY #2: MONEY / OR _____

1) _____

2) _____

3) _____

4) _____

5) _____

CATEGORY #3: EDUCATION / OR _____

1) _____

2) _____

3) _____

4) _____

5) _____

CATEGORY #4: SUPPORT OR _____

1) _____

2) _____

3) _____

4) _____

5) _____

CATEGORY #5: OTHER / OR _____

1) _____

2) _____

Cz the Day!

3) _____

4) _____

5) _____

Is your brain tired yet? No worries! You set the pace of your progress. When you start feeling drained, stop. When you are re-energized and re-focused, pick up where you left off.

Chapter 6

S o, let's review just how far you've come. You have created a Master list of all the things to be done to complete your goal. You have sorted that list into categories. Lastly, you have prioritized the list by category and order sequence. Perfect, now you need to develop your timeline.

When would you like your goal completed by? How long will it take you to complete each category? How many days or weeks to complete each step? Let's take a look at the house example.

As you can see, I have re-ordered and re-prioritized my overall list. Now, I am just going to plug in how long I think it will take me to do each step. Then, I will work it backwards to come up with my timeline. At this point, I only know that I want to buy a house within the next year.

Cz the Day!

GOAL: BUY A HOUSE
    TARGET COMPLETION DATE: <u>1 YEAR</u>

  A. HOME SELECTION (RESEARCH)

      1) Find a neighborhood within   4 weeks
            10 minutes of school
      2) Determine where I want to live   3 months

  B. LOAN QUALIFICATION (OTHER)

      1) Down payment requirements   60 days
      2) Clean up my credit   180 days

  C. INCOME (MONEY)
      1) Have a better paying job   6 months
      2) Figure out a second source of income 9 months

Take a moment and plug in some general time periods as applicable to your list.

Chapter 7

Next, figure out the overall time you need to complete each category based on the step requiring the most amount of time:

GOAL: BUY A HOUSE

    TARGET COMPLETION DATE: <u>1 YEAR</u>

A. HOME SELECTION (RESEARCH)   <u>TARGET: 3 Months</u>

    1) Find a neighborhood within   4 weeks
        10 minutes of school
    2) Determine where I want to live   3 months

B. LOAN QUALIFICATION (OTHER)   <u>TARGET: 6 Months</u>
    1) Down payment requirements   60 days
    2) Clean up my credit   180 days

C. INCOME (MONEY)   <u>TARGET: 9 Months</u>
    1) Have a better paying job   6 months
    2) Figure out a second source of income-   9 months

All set? Great!

Chapter 8

Now, get out a calendar and convert that target date to an actual date:

GOAL: BUY A HOUSE

     TARGET COMPLETION DATE: <u>1 YEAR = 12/31</u>

A. HOME SELECTION (RESEARCH) <u>TARGET: 3 Months = 3/31</u>
   1) Find a neighborhood 10 minutes of school   4 weeks
   2) Determine where I want to live   3 months

B. LOAN QUALIFICATION (OTHER) <u>TARGET: 6 Months = 6/30</u>
   1) Down payment requirements   60 days
   2) Clean up my credit   180 days

C. INCOME (MONEY)   <u>TARGET: 9 Months = 9/30</u>
   1) Have a better paying job   6 months
   2) Figure out a second source of income   9 months

Now you are getting it! So, go ahead and put an actual completion date by each step.

Chapter 9

When you are done, you will have completed your action plan which will look something like this:

GOAL: BUY A HOUSE

TARGET COMPLETION DATE: <u>YEAR = 12/31</u>

   A. HOME SELECTION (RESEARCH) <u>TARGET: 3 Months = 3/31</u>
      1) Find a neighborhood within   4 weeks = 1/31
         10 minutes of school
      2) Determine where I want to live   3 months = 3/31

   B. LOAN QUALIFICATION (OTHER) <u>TARGET: 6 Months = 6/30</u>
      1) Down payment requirements   60 days = 3/01
      2) Clean up my credit   180 days = 6/30

   C. INCOME (MONEY)   <u>TARGET: 9 Months = 9/30</u>
      1) Have a better paying job   6 months = 6/30
      2) Figure out a second source of income 9 mo = 9/30

Chapter 10

GOAL ACTION PLAN

GOAL: _____

TARGET DATE _____

CATEGORY #1: RESEARCH / OR _____

TARGET DATE _____

1) _____   _____

2) _____   _____

3) _____   _____

4) _____   _____

5) _____   _____

Cz the Day!

CATEGORY #2: MONEY / OR _____

TARGET DATE _____

1) _____   _____

2) _____   _____

3) _____   _____

4) _____   _____

5) _____   _____

CATEGORY #3: EDUCATION / OR _____

TARGET DATE _____

1) _____   _____

2) _____   _____

3) _____   _____

4) _____   _____

5) _____   _____

CATEGORY #4: SUPPORT / OR _____

TARGET DATE _____

1) _____   _____

2) _____   _____

3) _____   _____

4) _____   _____

5) _____   _____

CATEGORY #5: OTHER OR _____

TARGET DATE _____

1) _____   _____

2) _____   _____

3) _____   _____

4) _____   _____

5) _____   _____

Conclusion

There are six modules in the **Simple C Success System**©. In this module, you have just completed the 3rd C = **COURSE**. Many find this module the most intense. However, by completing the included exercises, you will have created an action plan and charted your **COURSE** to success.

You have at your fingertips the map to get you from where you are to where you want to be. As with most journeys, you may experience some road blocks and have to take a detour. Or you may come across an interesting area and decide to stay a while and check that place out before you continue to your final destination.

Your life is an adventure! Staying open to the possibilities and experiences along your way is part of the process. If at some point, you feel as if you have taken the "wrong road", look to your map to help you get back on track.

Cz the Day!

When you come to a crossroads, you may start to doubt your sense of direction. That is when it is important that you proceed with the 4th C = **COURAGE**. I wish you safe travels on your journey to success!

Module 4

COURAGE

Introduction

L et's face it, making a change in your life, no matter how much you desire the change, is scary. Change means to make a leap into the unknown in the hopes that there is something bigger, better or at the very least different from what you have now.

Even when you have figured out what you want (Module 1: **CLARITY**) and why you want it (Module 2: **CONFIDENCE**), even when you have developed your action plan (Module 3: **COURSE**), taking the necessary steps to move you forward takes **COURAGE**. An inner strength and resolve to move towards the life you desire to live.

In Module 3: **COURSE**, you created a path to get you where you want to be. What we didn't talk about was how to take that all important first step on this path. Sometimes I meet with potential clients who say to me "if I knew what to do, don't you think I'd be doing it?" And, my answer is "not necessarily".

Some people may be perceived as born risk-takers while even more are classified as risk-adverse. I believe the difference is in how badly you want the desired outcome. Is your goal a "need to have" or a "want to have" for you?

If your desire is an absolute NEED to have, but you are having doubts whether you can, should or will achieve what you desire then read Module 4: **COURAGE**. In this module, we will talk about ways to build your **COURAGE** so that you can indeed live a life you love.

Chapter 1

Think back to the story of the Wizard of Oz and the character of the Cowardly Lion. I can still picture the scene where he has wrapped himself in a cloak of flowers with a broken flower pot on his head as a crown, preening as King of the Forest. He was verbally challenging himself to be bold like an elephant or a rhinoceros, then at the very end, he asks and "what have I not got that they all got?" And, the answer was . . . **COURAGE!**

Just as with the other modules, this module will include some exercises to help you be courageous. Unlike the other modules, facing your fears can be the most difficult. Our personal feelings and events – what we have heard, read, imagined or experienced – have shaped a perception into a reality in our own minds.

Let's take a simple example. Maybe you were told over and over again as a child that children should be seen and not heard. This was a form of conditioning of our behavior to please our parents. Now as an adult it is hard for you to speak up to your parents. Even though you are no longer a child, you fall back into familiar habits.

Or, you came from a background where money was tight and little luxuries were viewed as wasteful. Now, even though you make a nice salary, you have trouble spending money on something for yourself because you don't really need it.

All I am saying is that our fears are based on our "perceptions becoming reality". In this module, let's explore some ways to change the perception that matters the most – yours.

Chapter 2

et's start with making a list of your top fears. Take a moment and go back and look at your Soul Goal™ from Module 2. Read it out loud to yourself, then list all the reasons why you "couldn't, wouldn't, shouldn't" get what you want. (i.e. start your own business, buy a new house, take the kids to Disney World, retire at 55 . . .) Get all those thoughts out of your head and onto the paper. Come on, in the back of your mind there are some lingering doubts that you can't have whatever it is you desire. So, out with it, what are they?

My Top 10 Fears are:

1) _____

2) _____

3) _____

4) _____

5) _____

6) _____

7) _____

8) _____

9) _____

10) _____

Good! Now doesn't it feel better to get them out of your head? I know it was a relief for me and once I could truly admit my fears to myself, then I could start on getting rid of them.

Chapter 3

I don't know about you, but once I put my doubts on paper, a few things happened for me. First, as I already mentioned, it was a relief to get them out of my head. I spend a lot of time thinking, thinking and thinking things through. But I am always better prepared to do something with my thoughts once they are expressed on paper. Now my thought has become something tangible, some "thing" I can work with, because trust me when I say this, thoughts are things!!

You have probably heard the famous Henry Ford quote "Whether you think you can or think you can't, you are right." So let's focus on getting you to the point where you think you can.

Cz the Day!

The first thing I would like you to do is similar to what we did in Module 3: **COURSE**. You went through all the actions you needed to take to achieve your goal and categorized those actions. We are going to do the same with your doubts and fears.

I think you will find that most of your fears will fall into these 4 categories:

- Money
- Support
- Self-Belief
- Past Experiences

Here are some examples relative to starting your own business:

Money:

✿ I don't have the money to start a new business.

Support:

✿ Everyone is telling me I am foolish to leave my corporate job.

Self-Belief:

✿ I'm not sure I really can run my own business.

Past-Experiences:

✿ I had to close the last business I had because it wasn't making enough money.

✿

Take a moment now and categorize your list.

Chapter 4

Now, take another look at your list. Are there some things listed there that now that you see them on paper, you can simply just cross them off? I bet there are. Here is an example from my own list.

In Module 1: **CLARITY**, Success for me is:

The most important thing for me is living a life I love serving a purpose that matters to me. I am Happy, Healthy, Wealthy, and WISE. (Worthwhile, Inspired, Successful and Empowered)

In Module 2: **CONFIDENCE**, my Soul Goal™ is:

I am a creative, confident, intuitive woman who values integrity, respect and optimism in myself and others. Using my organizing, strategizing and teaching skills, my Soul Goal™ is to help empower other women while spending more time with my family.

Cz the Day!

In Module 3: **COURSE**, one of my Actions is:
To transition from my current lucrative career to Coaching full-time.

So, needless to say, based on my own situation, there were some fears around money and support:

Money:
❖ I won't be able to reproduce the same income with the new business.

Support:
❖ Will my marriage sustain another career transition?

Self-Belief:
❖ Will people want to hear what I have to say?

Past-Experiences:
❖ My last business failed during the recession.

Once I took a look at these fears on paper, I could then address them more analytically and determine which I could simply cross off and which I needed to address. For me, my list ended up like this:

Money:
❖ ~~I won't be able to reproduce the same income with the new business.~~

- I realized my new business doesn't need to produce the same income and I reminded myself that I have always had the ability to find a job or another way to make additional income if needed.

Support:
- ~~Will my marriage sustain another career transition?~~
    - Answer: yes. My husband has supported me in the past and there is no reason to believe he wouldn't this time around.

Self-Belief:
- Will people want to hear what I have to say?
    - I didn't know so this stayed on my list.

Past-Experiences:
- ~~My last business failed during the recession.~~
    - After more consideration, I reconciled that it was the business that failed and not me; which made me realize I was ready to start another new business.

I encourage you at this stage to spend some time with your own list and see if there are any items that can be crossed off. When you are done, please write out your updated list by categories. We will then address each category in turn.

Chapter 5

MONEY FEARS:

1) _____

2) _____

3) _____

SUPPORT FEARS:

1) _____

2) _____

3) _____

SELF-BELIEF FEARS:

1) _____

Cz the Day!

2) _____

3) _____

PAST EXPERIENCES FEARS:

1) _____

2) _____

3) _____

Chapter 6

Money! Money! Money! Money! Why does so much of what we fear have to do with money???? Is it because we have been taught that "money is the root of all evil"? Is it that "money cannot buy happiness"? Somewhere along the line it became wrong to want to have money. Personally, I believe that there is nothing wrong with wanting, having, even spending money. Remember what we spoke about in the first and second modules: CLARITY and CONFIDENCE? Know what you want and why you want it. If what you want is directly related to your core values, then how can money not be a good thing??

Ok, enough of that rant, because in this module, COURAGE, the fear is not in making and having money, but is in not having enough money in the first place to do what you want to do to live a life you love living.

Cz the Day!

That ole "it takes money to make money" theory. As far as that goes, not having enough money as a Fear Factor is just a circumstance that needs to be addressed.

So here are some ways to Courageously address your Money Fears:

1. Getting Money
   - Obtain some investors (get creditworthy)
   - Ask family and/or friends for a loan
   - Use a credit card

2. Making Money
   - Sell some "stuff"
   - Find a second job
   - Perform a service

3. Having Money
   - Value yourself and your services
   - Recognize that money received for service is well-deserved

For the record, lack of money has never been a stop-gap for me. When I truly needed an investment source, I found it. Sometimes using conventional methods, sometimes using creative methods. Money is a tangible fear.

Chapter 7

Achieving your goals will not happen overnight. It takes time and patience. It will not be unusual for friends and family, those you turn to for Support, to question your decisions. Back in Module 1 we had an exercise to prepare you for these types of questions. As you move forward towards your goals, you may want to review your responses from that exercise.

Keep in mind that friends and family may just be plain scared for you! They feel they are being supportive when they are telling you cautionary tales. They have no idea how these tales can and will affect you. After all, they just have your best interests at heart. Right? Maybe yes and maybe no.

If not having a Support System is one of your fears, the good news is you can address this concern by getting a new support system. Sometimes when our lives take on a new direction, we need to find new friends and like-minded individuals. Check for local MeetUp Groups or even online support groups that are attuned with your cause. Coaches will frequently offer group coaching sessions or even a monthly support gathering.

Chapter 8

Dealing with our own Self-Limiting Beliefs can be the most difficult of fears to address. Changing a mindset is like creating a new habit. It generally takes at least 30 days of consistent, repetitive behavior. Having a daily mantra or affirmation is a tool that helps; along with furthering our education.

It can be hard to excel at something you have never done before. For instance, I mentioned earlier that one of my fears relative to self-belief is:

❖ Will people want to hear what I have to say?

When I really thought about this question, I realized it had more to do with my fear of speaking publically. I am very comfortable with who I am and what I have to say, just not with saying it to others in a larger forum. In fact, since I am a teacher, I find that if I "trick my mind" into telling myself I am teaching a class, I do just fine.

 Cz the Day!

Here are some other Mind Tips for Working Through Your Fears:

- Expect the best
- Get comfortable with fear
- Keep positive thoughts
- Don't give fear any of your time or energy
- Remember your successes
- Ask for encouragement
- Believe in yourself

Chapter 9

For some of us, Past Experiences may be the easiest fear to get through, for others the hardest. You may recall in the **Simple C Success System**© Introduction I mentioned that I am very good at leaving the past in the past. I have to share, though, that this was a learned response.

I used to be pretty hard on myself if/when things did not turn out the way that I had hoped. Always wanting to know what I had done wrong, why my efforts weren't good enough. It took a while for me to realize that life happens and goes on, and that I prefer to not dwell in the past but to move forward towards the future.

So, I do still spend some time evaluating the past situation and trying to figure out the associated life lesson, but now I give myself a time period (which varies based on the situation) then I move on. Now that doesn't mean that I forget, it means that I forgive, mainly, myself. That, my friends, was the hardest lesson to learn. To stop beating myself up for past choices and decisions. What's done is done. Learn from this past experience and move on.

What has helped me to gain some closure is to physically symbolize the end of the past. For instance:

- When a relationship ended badly, I put all the remembrances in a cigar box, nailed it shut like a coffin complete with epitaph and "cremated" it in the fireplace while playing Elton John' funeral for a friend. (True story!!)

- When a desired career change came to fruition, on little pieces of paper I wrote all the things people had said about why I couldn't do what I was about to do, and froze them in an old fashioned ice cube tray. When they were solid ice, I pulverized them in the garbage disposal and washed them down the drain.

- If I am having self-doubts before a speaking engagement, I might take a moment before I leave for the venue to blow all these fears into a balloon and let it go. Again to get the fear out of mind.

Chapter 10

I f you are still struggling with finding the **COURAGE** to move confidently in the direction of your dreams, try this exercise I call the Simple Process for Putting Risk into Perspective:

Step 1: Write Down Your <u>Main Concern</u>

_____

_____

_____

_____

Step 2: List the <u>Issues</u> Related to this Concern:

_____

Cz the Day!

_____

_____

_____

Step 3: List the <u>Desired Outcomes:</u>

_____

_____

_____

_____

Step 4: List your <u>Fears</u> about this Concern:

_____

_____

_____

_____

Step 5: List your <u>Available Resources:</u>

_____

_____

_____

_____

Step 6: Write the Worst Thing that Could Happen:

_____

_____

_____

_____

RISK CALCULATOR:

If you can live with the answer to Step 6 - take the chance!
If you cannot, then you may need to seek further **CLARITY**
and re-explore your definition of success.

Conclusion

When talking about **COURAGE** it is important to realize that some people are just as afraid of Success as they are of Failure. With great success, comes great responsibility. I just want to take a moment to remind you, I am only interested in your definition of success. If you are truly in tune with that definition, then you will find the courage to do the things you need to do.

Some people say I give the impression of being fearless because I am generally willing to try something new. Of course, that is not true. It is just that when my desire outweighs my reluctance, I do the things I need to do anyway!! Just as you can.

Cz the Day!

If we are to actually achieve the success we desire, though, we also need to be committed to our goals and to ourselves. Continue on to Module 5: **COMMITMENT** for tips and tricks to hold ourselves accountable to living a life we love.

Module
5
COMMITMENT

Introduction

COMMITMENT: a promise and/or obligation. In our last module, we looked at ways to confront and address our fears. Making a commitment, even to ourselves, is taking on a big responsibility. When you hear the word commitment, what comes to mind?

Do you view the word as relative to a commitment to others? As in being responsible for the welfare of others – such as in a marriage? Or do you like the idea of that type of bond? You will either have the fear of taking on the obligation or prefer the assurance that the promise will be kept.

In this module, you will be asked to make a **COMMITMENT** to yourself; your goals, dreams, desires. If you are not totally committed, then it will be easy to walk away or make excuses when the path chosen and outlined does not go 100% according to plan. The one guarantee?

Cz the Day!

Things will not go 100% according to plan.

So now let's explore what to do when life interferes with your best-laid plans.

Chapter 1

The first thing I want you to do is to go back to the very beginning and remind yourself:

What is your definition of success?

_____

_____

_____

_____

Why is achieving this success important to you?

_____

_____

Cz the Day!

Good! Now let's test your definition to be sure it is right for you.

Ask yourself these five questions:

1) Does it give me life?
   Do you feel happy and excited when thinking about how your life will be when your success is achieved?

2) Does this definition of success align with my core values?
   Is what you want in sync with your principles and beliefs?

3) Does it cause me to grow?
   Will you need to stretch yourself to become more than you currently know how to be?

4) Do you need help to achieve your success?
   Do you need further insight and guidance to create the life you are imagining?

5) Does it have some good in it for others?
   Will achieving success have a positive impact on my family, friends, community, someone other than myself?

If you have answered "yes" to all of the above questions, then what you desire has the momentum to pull you forward. If you had some hesitancy in your answers, you may want to go back to Module 1: **CLARITY** and further refine what a life you would love living looks like for you.

Simply put, you need to be so in tune with the life you want that you can no longer imagine living your current life. If that is where you are at, say, "I'm in!! I'm all in and ready to do this! I'm ready to live a life I love!"

Really? Then it is time to Commit with a capital C. Time to sign your name and make a contract with yourself.

Yes! I am ready to achieve my definition of success and live a life I love:

Signature: _____

Date: _____

Chapter 2

Wow! That's a biggie. Really committing to making a change. To do the work, to be persistent and diligent in moving forward in the direction of your dream – one day at a time.

Back in Module 3: **COURSE**, you came up with an action plan complete with due dates. If you skipped that module, this would be a good time to go through the worksheets and develop your plan. Having your roadmap to success, listing the actual steps that need to be taken to achieve your goals, is crucial.

When you developed the plan, you broke down each of the four major goals (Health/Well-Being, Love/Relationships, Career/Vocation, Time/Money Freedom) into more manageable steps and mini-steps complete with deadlines. Now would be a good time to pull out that plan.

 Cz the Day!

I realize that viewing everything it will take to reach your goals can be daunting. So, at this point, you can decide if you want to work by "goal" or by "dates". Meaning, do you want to choose just one goal to work on right now? Or, do you want to work on multiple goals simultaneously? For illustration purposes of this chapter, we will work on just one goal – the one that is the most important to you at this time.

Now take a look at that goal and the steps that need to be taken and write down the mini-steps in chronological order. Going back to the example in Module 3, Chapter 9 my list looked like this:

GOAL: BUY A HOUSE
    TARGET COMPLETION DATE: <u>YEAR = 12/31</u>

  A. HOME SELECTION (RESEARCH) <u>TARGET: 3 Months = 3/31</u>
      1) Find a neighborhood 10 minutes of school 4 weeks =1/31
      2) Determine where I want to live   3 months = 3/31

  B. LOAN QUALIFICATION (OTHER) <u>TARGET: 6 Months = 6/30</u>
      1) Down payment requirements   60 days = 3/01
      2) Clean up my credit   180 days = 6/30

  C. INCOME (MONEY)   <u>TARGET: 9 Months = 9/30</u>
      1) Have a better paying job   6 months = 6/30
      2) Figure out a second source of income   9 mo = 9/30

In chronological order, my list would now look like:

Find a neighborhood	4weeks	1/31
Down payment requirements	60 days	3/01
Determine where I want to live	3 months	3/31
Clean up my credit	180 days	6/30
Have a better paying job	6 months	6/30
Figure out a second source of income		
	9 months	9/30

The next step, is to put these dates on your calendar. **COMMIT** to having completed the action item by the target date. Tell someone your plan, ask them to hold you accountable to these dates. It is now time to work the plan.

NOTE TO SELF: If you miss a deadline, do not give up! Set a new deadline. Re-commit to your goal.

Chapter 3

What? Progress isn't happening fast enough? Seeking immediate results? Looking for shortcuts? Well, I didn't say that the process for creating a life you love was "easy". I said it was "simple". You still need to do the work.

I know. I know. We live in a world of instant gratification. But, isn't it gratifying to know that if you continue to move along the path, you will eventually reach your destination?

Not good enough you say? Then, be sure to reward yourself and celebrate every little success. You found the area where you want to buy your house? High five!! Drive through it every now and then and remind yourself why you are paying down your current debts and cleaning up your credit.

Relook at your vision board and re-affirm that you truly desire to live the life you have envisioned for yourself.

Cz the Day!

Repeat a daily affirmation that speaks to already achieving your goals. Something like "I am so happy and grateful to be living in the neighborhood with the best schools for my kids".

These little celebrations and reminders help keep us on track and moving forward in the direction of our dreams. Keep a positive attitude, know that you can have the life you desire.

Chapter 4

U h Oh!! Life took an unexpected turn. You thought you aced the job interview only to have the position offered to someone else. You need to meet one more contingency before your business loan will be approved. Someone outbid you on the house you wanted to buy. Now what?

I find it is helpful to have the attitude of "This or something better". It is easy to get frustrated or disappointed when something we have been working so diligently towards doesn't happen the way we planned. When it feels like we have taken two steps forward to move three steps back.

But think back to other similar experiences you had that have gotten you to where you are today. Perhaps your high school sweetheart that you thought you were going to spend the rest of your life with, ended up marrying someone else. Years later you find out that he has struggled through several divorces;

while you and the man you did marry, adore each other and the family you have created together.

Or, that the company where you really wanted to work was later bought out and all the employees were then laid off. While you were able to rapidly move up the corporate ladder at your current company. When "life happens" it helps to trust that you are exactly where you are supposed to be.

We all know that hindsight is a wonderful teacher. But so is intuition and anticipation. Don't let what may be perceived as a setback, set you back. Re-commit and continue moving forward.

Chapter 5

In the last chapter, we spoke about keeping a positive attitude when situations arise that are out of our control. In this chapter, let's take those situations that arise that you can do something about. Like, you find that you need another $2000 for the down payment of your house. Or, your business idea is not deemed financially feasible. When these type of things happen, it is time to get creative. To explore your options, and trust me when I say, there are always options.

With the down payment example:
- How can you come up with the extra money? (garage sale, sell the unused china, etc.)
- Can the price of the house be lowered to accommodate your finances?
- Will the current owners do a short-term carry-back loan?

With the business idea example:
- Is there more information that needs to be included in your business plan?
- Who else do you need to talk to about your business idea?
- Is there some professional that will endorse your idea to gain credibility?

You get the concept. What other steps can you take to get to a "yes"? Nobody likes hearing the word no. I suggest you find out the underlying reason for the no, so the objections can be addressed. Like already mentioned, if you want something bad enough, you will figure out a way to get it.

Chapter 6

Excuse me?? Hello?? What have you done today to move you in the direction of the life you want to live? Nothing?!! Is there seriously nothing you can do today? What do you mean you will work on your action plan tomorrow? This isn't Tara! Do you want all your hopes and dreams to be Gone with the Wind? I didn't think so!

I don't care if all you are doing is thinking about different ways to achieve your goal, the main thing is to keep your goal first and foremost in your mind – <u>every day</u> – and do something.

If your goal is to start your own business, it can be making a phone call to a potential client, doing some research about how to use social media, attending a networking event. If your goal is to change jobs, it can be updating your resume, looking online for today's job postings, seeking a letter of recommendation from a business associate.

Cz the Day!

For days when you feel like procrastinating, and that is what you are doing, putting off what needs to be done, it is helpful to keep a list of at least 20 Ideas that will move you forward. This list can be ideas that you just jot down when inspiration hits. Some ideas will only take a minute or two to accomplish, some will take longer.

Again, the point is to do something. Even if it is to look at the list and choose one item to do tomorrow. Are you getting the point here? Keep focused on your goal. Do not put off until tomorrow what can be done today. Do you want to be in the same place you are now next year or the year after? No? I didn't think so . . .

Chapter 7

E arlier in this module, I mentioned that it can be helpful to have someone hold you accountable to your goals/dreams/plans. Let's take a moment and talk about that more in depth. When you have a goal to lose weight and commit to going to the gym three times a week, is it easier to go by yourself or with a friend; someone else who is determined to be at their ideal weight? With a friend, of course.

We may be willing to talk ourselves out of going and let our self down, but if we know someone is there waiting for us, it is not as easy to not show up as we don't want to let them down. That friend is there to lend support and also to remind us of our COMMITMENT.

It is very important when creating a life we love, to have someone hold us accountable to moving forward. As we discussed in Module 4: COURAGE, having someone support our efforts helps us feel good about what we are working

to achieve. An Accountability Partner, however, is there to keep you on track.

Whereas your support group might sympathize with disappointments and missed deadlines, an Accountability Partner is going to push you to set a new deadline. If you have a naturally competitive nature, accountability can come in the form of an online group that posts their weekly progress. Watching someone achieve their goals faster than you can spur you on to meet your own deadlines.

If you are not competitive, however, a group like this may have the opposite effect. Leaving you feeling that you "always come in last". So it is important to pick the right partner for you. The attributes of an Accountability Partner include: respect, open-mindedness, support, confidentiality, and compassionate honesty. Think about your circle of influence and determine if you already know someone who could fill that role for you. If so, great!! Go ahead and ask them if they are willing to be your Accountability Partner.

If not, you may want to hire a Coach as this is typically one of the roles they can fill on your path to success. In order to move more expediently towards living a life you love, it is important to have an accountability partner to remind you of your **COMMITMENT**.

Conclusion

When you think about successful people and their common characteristics, one of the highest on the list is **COMMITMENT**. To not stop until they achieve the success they desire.

- Thomas Edison failed over 1000 times before successfully creating a light bulb.
- Walt Disney was told "he lacked imagination and good ideas".
- Oprah was "deemed unfit for TV."
- Albert Einstein was "thought to be mentally challenged".
- Lucille Ball was considered "a failed B-movie star".

So I challenge you to commit to creating a life you love each and every day. Then, before long, you will actually be living that life.

Throughout **Cz the Day!** you have been walking through the **Simple C Success System©**. And, yes, everything may sound good to you in theory. You may have even done all the exercises and

Cz the Day!

are ready to embark on your journey. Or, you may be feeling a little overwhelmed with the process. If that is the case, in the next module we will explore the benefits of having a **COACH.**

Module 6

COACH

Introduction

There are all types of Coaches out in the world today. Business, Career, Life, Success, etc. But what exactly does a **COACH** do? I get this question quite often. You have probably heard of the coaching profession. You may even have a friend or family member that is a coach. But still you don't know what exactly they do. I know because I have been a coach for close to 20 years and my family still wonders what it is that I "do".

In this module, we will explore the profession of Coaching and the role a Coach can play in helping you live a life you love. We will also explore how to choose the right **COACH** for you.

Chapter 1

So let's start with how I found out about coaching myself. Back in the early 90's I found myself in a place I really did not want to be. I was the classic case of Smart Woman, Stupid Choices. Can any of you relate to that?

My nice independent life was cruising along just fine until I met a man that I thought was my soul mate. Attractive, ambitious and best of all wanted me!! So we hook up. I sell my house, leave my job to be with him and start a business together in another state.

Fast forward to the next year (yes it didn't take long) and I find myself out of money, alienated from my friends, far removed from my family and totally dependent on this man who was quite honestly not treating me very well. In fact, I was beginning to think I was crazy, because although he treated me well out in public, behind closed doors he was "meaner

than a snake" as they say in the south (where this original CA girl was living at that time!)

By the time I had had enough, I had no clue how to get back to being me. And, my self-esteem was so long gone, I couldn't even fathom that I had a choice in the matter. All I knew was that I needed to talk to someone to help me figure it out. But, I didn't know who to talk to.

I knew I didn't want to talk to the pastor; didn't want to air any dirty laundry where it could ruin the "image". I didn't want to talk to a counselor or a therapist – I had no interest in talking about how I got to this place or even why. I just wanted to get out of my situation.

Luckily, I still had one friend that I would talk to on the sly that my very controlling partner did not know about. And she is the one that pointed me in the direction of a Life Coach to gain some perspective on my particular situation. I honestly had no idea there was even such a profession as Coaching. But what a difference that coach made in my life!

Chapter 2

The first thing that **COACH** offered me was some **CLARITY**. By now you all know that Clarity is part of the Simple C Success System©. A coach can help you clear all the clutter in your mind to see the true picture of what you really want. With a coach, you do not focus on your past, but you focus on your future and what you want your life to be.

The 2nd C is **CONFIDENCE**. My self-esteem was so stripped down I couldn't even remember who I was anymore. So, I had to rediscover me. What is it I truly care about? What do I value about myself? Then once I discovered what I truly wanted and why, I needed a plan.

I needed the 3rd C – a **COURSE** of action. What are the steps I need to take to get me from where I am today to where I want to be? Whew! Working with a coach takes work, I thought – but I knew in my heart I wanted this new

life I was envisioning.

But, change is scary!! I wanted that new life, I could see that it was possible, but I became afraid – afraid of starting again on my own. So I had to have **COURAGE** the 4th C. When a fear came up, my Coach would help talk me through the perceived obstacle. Because fear is based on my own perception of the situation. Once I changed my attitude, I found I was able to move forward and face my fears.

I then made a **COMMITMENT**, the 5th C, to my new goals and objectives. And, if I became complacent or lazy my **COACH** was there to be my Accountability Partner. Checking in with me to be sure I stayed on track.

My **COACH**, the 6th C, also became my Mentor supporting me all the way through the process. Walking beside me every step of the way. I didn't have to go it alone. I had the support I needed. Someone who believed in me sometimes more than I believed in myself. And, who cheered and celebrated my successes along the way.

Chapter 3

So, what exactly does a **COACH** do? A Coach is a professional that works closely with people to help them live their lives to the fullest potential. We help people identify, set and achieve goals in any aspect of their lives, including: health, relationships, career, business, time and money.

Sometimes I find that when people are asking me what I do, they really want to know "how" a coach helps clients. And that how will vary from coach to coach. The one consistency is that Coaching is typically conducted through a series of sessions conducted either in person, over the telephone or virtually using Skype or Google Hangouts. The length and content of these sessions will be based on individual client needs.

Each coach will have their own set of processes and programs that they use to help their clients. Through my book **Cz the Day!** you have learned the basis of my coaching practice, the **Simple C Success System©**: **Clarity, Confidence, Course, Courage, Commitment** and **Coach.**

Chapter 4

Imagine if you will that you are Dorothy in the Wizard of Oz. You wake up one day and realize you are not in Kansas anymore and you need to get home. This is not the life you imagined you would be living. Your "home" may be to change your career, start your own business or find the love of your life. Fill in the blank for yourself.

Then, when you landed in Oz, you met Glinda the Good Witch and she helped you **Clarify** what it is you wanted then guides you to a path. She points out the **Course** of the yellow brick road. And on that road, you will have to have **Courage**. You will run into your share of thrown apples and flying monkeys along the way, but you are **Committed** to getting to the Wizard in order to get home.

You can clearly see your family and friends wondering where you are and when you would be getting back. So even though you are fearful of what would find out from OZ, you take some time to gain some **Confidence** by grooming yourself and dressing for success in preparation for your return. You thought you were ready, you made it to Oz - but then life threw you some curve balls.

In order to get home, you had to get the witches broom. There always seems to be a setback along your path to success, but just like Dorothy you have to remind yourself of what you truly want and recommit to the plan. And, even when you are finally on your way, you made it into that hot air balloon and were taking off – one more challenge happened. And the balloon sailed on without you.

Then, just when you thought all was lost, Glinda your **Coach** reappeared and reminded you that you already have everything you need within you to get back home. You just had to believe in the power of your dream; your definition of success. That there really is no place like home. Or that your idea can be a successful business. Or that you can make an extra $1000 needed to take your kids to Disney World. Or whatever it is you truly want.

You see, I believe we all have much more potential than we realize. I also believe that we all deserve to live a life we love living. A **COACH** can help you design and define your life so you can achieve the success you desire, just as my coach did for me all those many years ago.

Chapter 5

So, now you may be thinking, "OK so maybe I could use a **COACH**, but how do I find one?" Well, you could ask around and see if anyone you know has worked with a coach they would recommend. You could go online and search for one. You could even call your local chamber for a referral. Then once you get some names and numbers, you will want to talk to them and find out more about their services. Most coaches will offer a free consultation or even a free session.

You will want to ask your perspective coach a few questions besides their program fee. For instance:

- What is their coaching philosophy?
- What is their coaching experience?
- Are they credentialed and if so, through who?
- What is their coaching specialty?
- What is their coaching process?

- And, this is key, <u>any other question that is important to you</u>.

Then, once you get off the phone, you need to ask yourself these questions:

- What was your comfort level talking to the coach?

- Did you connect?

- Were you able to ask everything you wanted to know or did they control the conversation? Only talk about themselves and their program?

- Compared to all the coaches you spoke with, who understood best where you are and where you want to be?

- Which coach did you feel would inspire you to take the actions necessary to accomplish your goals?

- And, whose program best fit your needs and reason for hiring a coach in relation to training, experience, process, and price?

Remember that change does not happen overnight. You will be establishing a relationship with your coach and you want to choose the right coach for you.

Conclusion

As I mentioned, coaches come in all shapes, sizes, specialties. Working with a coach will accelerate the process for achieving the success you desire. You can work with a coach on a one-on-one basis or you can choose to participate in group sessions.

If you decide to work with a **COACH**, I congratulate you on making an investment in yourself. You are worth it!!

Simple C Success System©

Clarity:
Know how you define success and what goals are important to you.

Confidence:
Identify who you are, your core values, and be sure your goals are in alignment.

Course:
Develop an action plan with the steps and deadlines needed to accomplish your goals.

Courage:
Be able to ask for the help you need or do what scares you anyway.

Commitment:
Come up with solutions to situations as they arise. Figure out a way to make it happen.

Coach:
Have someone who believes in you, inspires you, empowers you and mentors you to success!

Celebration

CZ THE DAY!

Cz the Day!

I have enjoyed our time together walking through the six modules of the **Simple C Success System**©. Throughout the program, there has been one main constant – you: your desire, your values, your knowledge, your faith, trust and belief in yourself. This book is a vehicle for you to express what it is you really want in life and come up with a plan, or blueprint, for how you can move you from where you are today to where you truly want to be.

The second constant was the use of the letter C in the Success System so you can create the life you would love to be living. Now it is time to embark on your journey and as you start down your chosen path to success, as you get ready to **Cz the Day!,** I would like to share some other C's that may help you along your way.

Character

So often if we choose to create a better life for ourselves, we can be perceived as selfish. I disagree. One of the guiding principles of the Simple C is "is there any good in this for others?" We discussed how having money for money's sake serves no one. It is what you do with your money that makes the difference between selfishness and selflessness.

We have already talked about the importance of being committed to your goals. We went through an exercise to get you prepared for those expressing concern over your choices. But we didn't really talk about how to build a barrier and protect yourself from these "dream killers".

The bottom line is that while you maintain your character you may need to disassociate or disconnect from those who it does not serve you to be around. We have a tendency to want to justify our choices, but truly we do not need to. As long as you are comfortable and confident that you are making the right choice for you, that is all that matters.

Considerate

Kindness will also go a long way in moving you along your path. I do not subscribe to "winning at all costs". There is no need for competition when you feel that there is enough for everyone. I know it can be hard to be gracious when someone else gets whatever it is you want before you, but have faith that something better will show up for you instead. If it is you who gets what you want, be considerate and mindful of those striving to be like you. Carry yourself with dignity and grace and never be demeaning of others.

Common Sense

When we have a plan together, it is natural to be excited to move forward. We sometimes rush out the gate to achieve our goals. I just want to caution you here to use your common sense. Take calculated risks. For instance instead of using all your savings to enroll in a new marketing program, take the payment plan option or use only a portion that will not put your bank account in jeopardy.

Cheerful

When the going gets tough, stay cheerful. Know that this too shall pass. Keeping optimist helps you to find the reasons to keep on going. Besides others prefer to work with and do business with those that are congenial rather than those who are not.

Challenges

Everyone faces challenges in life now and again. It is how you confront each issue that will make all the difference. Look for the opportunity that the situation is presenting for you to better yourself or actually improve your position based on the resolution.

Curiosity

Stay curious! Do not take generally accepted foregone conclusions as fact. Explore the "what ifs" and challenge yourself to find a better way or solution. Do not always accept "that's just the way it is". Look for ways to improve the situation.

Creativity

Being creative can make the difference between living the life you want to be living and giving up when life "happens". Thinking outside the box to figure out how to move you from where you are to where you want to be, will help you explore other avenues that may be just as satisfying if not more so that the original path.

Connections

We've all heard it said, "It's not what you know, it's who you know" and having the right connections can help you achieve your goals faster than going it alone. Strive to build reciprocal relationships. Willingly share your knowledge and resources with others, and they will do the same with you.

Celebrations

We sometimes get so caught up in checking the boxes off our "to do" lists that we forget to celebrate our mini-milestones along the way. These small celebrations remind us that we are moving forward and acknowledge our hard work and tenacity in the pursuit of our goals and dreams. Take a moment now and then to recognize just how far you have come!

Cz the Day!

As with most authors, I use writing as a creative vehicle to express myself. I want to take this moment to thank you for reading and participating in the **Simple C Success System©**. I hope it brings you as much success as it continues to bring to me.

And, finally, here are some last words of encouragement:

- Rise Above Your Circumstances
- Take a Chance!
- Make a Choice
- Stay Calm and Carry On
- Be Your Own Compass
- Find Creative Solutions
- Give Yourself Credit
- Change Your Perspective
- Challenge Yourself
- Celebrate Every Little Success

Cz the Day! ~ *Susan*

Need Help?

At U-SUCCEED, I specialize in working with clients who are seeking to achieve their personal and professional goals to enjoy a richer life experience.

Whether you are seeking the clarity, the confidence, the course or an accountability partner to achieve your dream, I can help! All of my clients are STARs – Striving Towards Amazing Results. If this is your time to pursue your goals so you can love your life, then I invite you to **Cz the Day!** Schedule a Complimentary Session today by contacting me through my website, **www.U-SUCCEED.com.**

After your session, should we decide that we are a good fit to work together, know that as your Success Coach and Mentor, I will Believe in U, Inspire U, Empower U and Mentor U to Success through your selected coaching program. You only have one life, make it a life you love living! I look forward to speaking with you soon. *Susan*

www.ingramcontent.com/pod-product-compliance
Lightning Source LLC
LaVergne TN
LVHW051508080426
835509LV00017B/1972